LOVE -YOUR- AGE, GIRL

Be Good to Yourself and Live to 100!

Inspirations, Hints, Tips, and Truths

Dr. Marilou Ryder
Jessica Thompson

Love Your Age, Girl

Paperback ISBN: 978-1-7356854-1-0
Kindle: 978-1-7356854-2-7
Library of Congress Control Number: 2020949064

Printed in the United States of America
Delmar Publishing, Huntington Beach, CA 92648

Book design by StoriesToTellBooks.com

LOVE YOUR AGE, GIRL

Be Good to Yourself and Live to 100!
Inspirations, Hints, Tips and Truths

Dr. Marilou Ryder
Jessica Thompson

INTRODUCTION

Love Your Age, Girl! What time is it? What day is it? What month is it? What year is it? How old am I? You know exactly how old you are, and if you don't love your age now, you will once you turn the pages. Loving your age is all about loving yourself. Loving yourself just the way you are. Not the way you were but precisely the way you are now. Yes, we may be a few pounds heavier, a few inches shorter, a few hairs whiter, but we have more wisdom, grace, confidence, strength, and perseverance than ever. Our shell may be more weathered, but our core is more robust and continues to define our worth. At our age, girls just want to have fun. We also want to enjoy a purpose and reason for being here. We want to share our worth and pass it on to others to reach the platform we are standing on.

Aging for women is a natural process that never seems to stand still. That is why we give you a chance to share with us some adult purpose and humor. We've gathered some of our best quotes and truths from our Ambassadors of Aging in the following pages.

What would aging be without taking a few chances and challenges? Our ***30-Day Challenge*** will encourage you to step out of your comfort zone and see what you can accomplish in 24 hours. ***Take a Chance*** with a few of our recommendations or make up some of your own. ***Take a Chance*** aims to encourage you to do something new and different. We have topped off our ***Love Your Age, Girl*** with ***Original Inspirations***, ***This or That***, and ***Martini Fantasies***. You will meet ***Frieda,*** our famous and fierce little texter. She is a hoot that will toot her bark and end with her bite.

Finally, we've put together our creative juices with some ***Womantoons***. We hope you find a few that will put a smile on your face. Enjoy our book and remember to ***Love Your Age, Girl***. Every Day!!!

*Love your age, know your worth, and
volunteer to make someone's life better!*

TAKE OUR
30-Day
Challenge

JESSICA & MARILOU

We challenge you to be good to yourself everyday! Try a new strategy for 30 days!

GOOD LUCK

!

TRIVIA

WHAT 75-YEAR-OLD CANCER SURVIVOR WAS THE FIRST BLACK WOMAN TO REACH THE NORTH POLE?

BARBARA HILLARY

#WISEWOMANTIPS

WHEN YOU THINK ABOUT THINGS YOU FEAR THE MOST THEY USUALLY DON'T HAPPEN. IF THEY HAVEN'T HAPPENED BY NOW, CHANCES ARE THEY WON'T.

... After retiring I struggled with a feeling of uselessness. I had to look back over my life to examine what made me engaged and feeling valued. Almost everyone I know has encountered this phenomenon after retiring. They say they want to feel important and want to contribute to something bigger than themselves. I now volunteer at a women's shelter and once again feel like I matter.

Bobbie (67)

LOVE YOUR AGE

**Don't give up.
Don't give in to
your aches and
pains.**

I believe the secret to a happy marriage is trying not to make one another into a person that they are not.

Katy Age 72

Woman's Best Friend

My dog is my lifeline. I live alone and when I wake up in the morning I like to talk but there's no one to talk to. Max, my dog listens intently and that's a real comfort for me as the days turn into weeks within the blink of an eye.

(Joan 89)

DAY 1
30-DAY CHALLENGE

PRACTICE
STANDING
ON ONE
FOOT
FOR 30
SECONDS

You still feel like a kid.

"

I found the older I got the less money I needed since I just about ran out of stuff I wanted or needed to buy.
(Joan 89)

DON'T LET ANYONE EVER MINIMIZE YOUR

 WORTH

I have read some type of book every day for as long as I can remember. I can be in 18th century England one day and the next day I'm on the streets of NYC. Reading has been my little secret.

Janis (88)

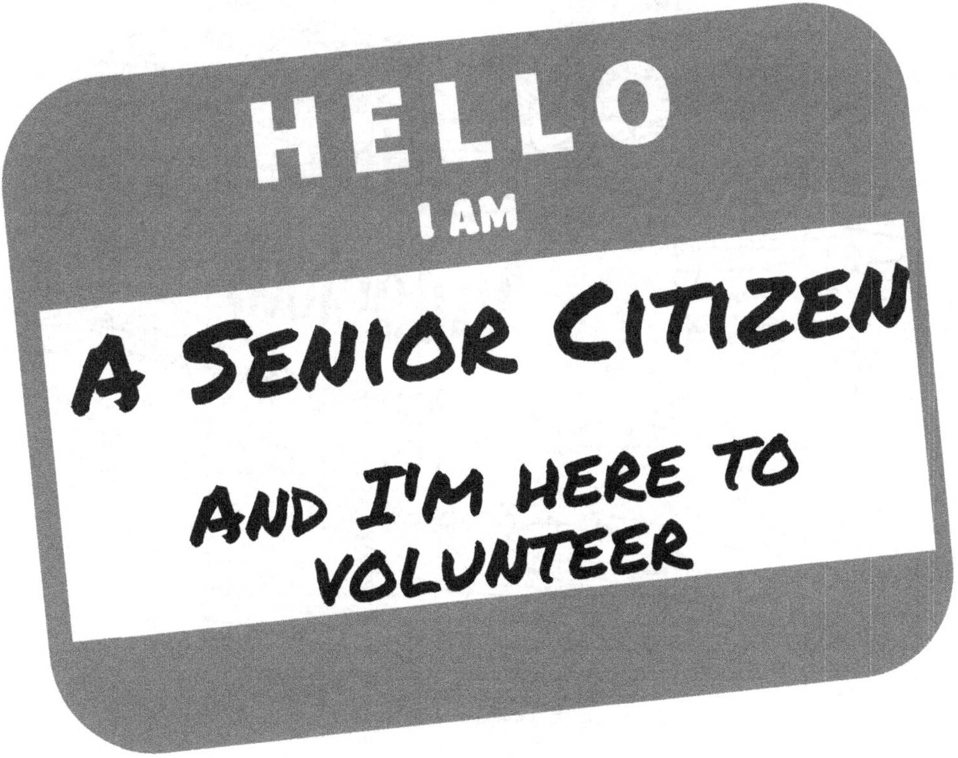
HELLO
I AM
A SENIOR CITIZEN
AND I'M HERE TO VOLUNTEER

DAY 2
30-DAY CHALLENGE

BEGIN
TAKING
A
DAILY
VITAMIN

Freida

I just sent my husband to the grocery store with a list of 25 items.

So, you needed some down time, huh?

It'll take him all day. I turn my phone off and get three hours to myself.

16

TAKE A CHANCE

Walk a mile every day.

#WISEWOMANTIPS

MAKE
A LOT
OF WOMAN
FRIENDS.

... I live alone and sometimes it can get plain lonely. One day I read in the paper that loneliness in older people can cause depression. Well, that's me. So what did I do? I took a big leap of faith and joined a few groups like a book club, the gym, and an art council. I should have been doing this all along but got caught up having a pity party.

Suzi (69)

POP QUIZ

What percent of women over 65 or older have Type 2 Diabetes?

A. 10 Percent

B. 25 Percent

C. 100 Percent

D. Under 5 Percent

Answer-A: According to the Mayo Clinic, since there is no cure for type 2 diabetes, losing weight, eating well, and exercising can help manage the disease.*

Cited from https://www.mayoclinic.org/diseases-conditions/type-2-diabetes/symptoms-causes/syc-20351193

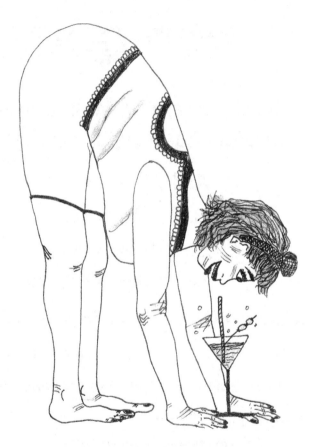

Dip and Sip! Dip and Sip! Carol wasn't going to let exercise cut into her Happy Hours.

MY MARTINI IS ALL
ABOUT THE 'ME' TIME
AND THE 'ME' TIME
AND GIVE ME
MORE OF THAT
'ME' TIME

DAY 3
30-DAY CHALLENGE

THROW OUT ALL YOUR EXPIRED FOODS

One day I added up all the hours I was watching TV and just about fell over. Monday-Friday I was watching 5 hours per day and weekends 6 hours for a total of 37 hours. I knew I had to do something because these numbers told me I was wasting my life. I made a rule... no more than 2 hours a day. That was really hard to do.

Beverly (68)

!

TRIVIA

WHAT 70-YEAR-OLD WOMAN RAN 7 MARATHONS ON 7 CONTINENTS IN 7 DAYS?

CHAU SMITH

LOVE YOUR AGE

Be proud of getting older because along with age comes wisdom.

This or That?

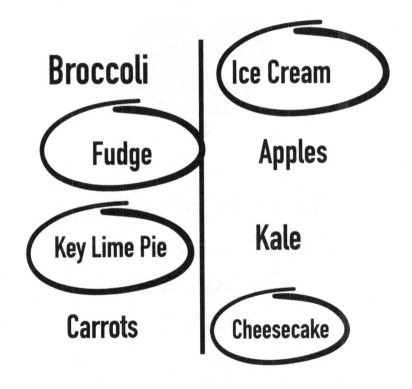

Broccoli | Ice Cream

Fudge | Apples

Key Lime Pie | Kale

Carrots | Cheesecake

DAY 4
30-DAY CHALLENGE

My husband and I retired at the same time. After we cleaned out the closets, remodeled the kitchen, and took three vacations we looked at one another and said, "Now what do we do?"

Katy Age 72

DON'T LET ANYONE EVER TELL YOU YOU'RE TOO OLD

You will sleep through the whole night without getting up to pee.

Stronger than Dirt

I am almost 90 years old and if there was one thing I would tell women to do would be to work out with some small barbells each day to build up the muscles in your arms. I feel almost as strong as I did 20 years ago. I can still carry 2-3 bags of groceries into the house. (Cindy 89)

DAY 5
30-DAY CHALLENGE

TOUCH YOUR TOES WITH BOTH HANDS 20 TIMES

#WISEWOMANTIPS

KEEP FRIENDS CLOSE. KEEP FAMILY CLOSER.

TAKE A CHANCE

Learn a new game such as Bridge, Mahjong, or Canasta.

... I walk every day, three to four miles. Even in the rain, I'm out walking. I've even got inclement weather gear just so I can walk. I am not balanced if I don't get that physical activity. And walking helps keep my back fluid so I don't get back pain.

Sandi (69)

POP QUIZ

What percent of women over 65 are obese?

A. 40 Percent

B. 11 Percent

C. 100 Percent

D. Too few to count

Answer-A: Obesity is a risk factor for diseases that are prevalent in older women, including cardiovascular disease, diabetes and some cancers. Exercise and a planned diet can help.

What's one piece of advice you would give an older woman?

Don't start dressing like an old lady.

Sarah (81)

DAY 6
30-DAY CHALLENGE

BUY
YOURSELF
SOME
FLOWERS

Don't think that gardening and learning to play the piano will satisfy all your needs after retiring especially if you have been in a high impact career. It felt like getting off a treadmill. I needed to reflect on who I was and what would make me feel valued.

Katy Age 72

Freida

You don't sound too chipper today.

I am so bored. I can't find anything productive to do.

Me too. I just ordered a Paint by Number kit on Amazon.

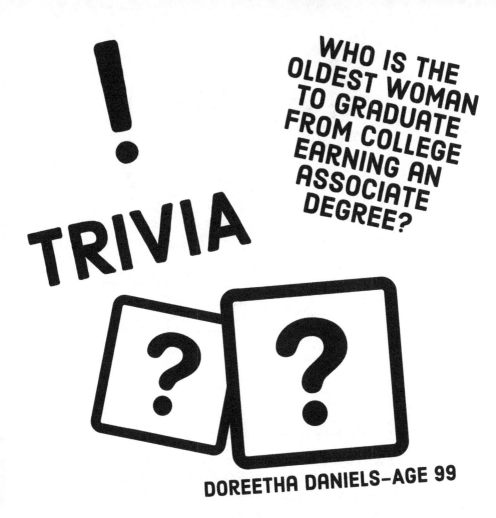

TRIVIA

WHO IS THE OLDEST WOMAN TO GRADUATE FROM COLLEGE EARNING AN ASSOCIATE DEGREE?

DOREETHA DANIELS—AGE 99

Liz was a bit nervous about her first virtual physical exam with Dr. Smith. In preparation, she had her hair styled and made sure her jewelry complemented her make-up.

LOVE YOUR AGE

Learn to deal with the bad days and be grateful for the good ones.

DAY 7
30-DAY CHALLENGE

GET
RID
OF ALL
YOUR
THROW
RUGS

... The one thing that concerns me the most as I age is my weight. I am probably 35-40 pounds overweight and I don't like that. I've got to put my nose to the grindstone to lose weight. I know I could do it easily but I would have to give up some of the pleasures I like so much. But this extra weight is killing me so I am going on a diet right now.

Sandi (69)

POP QUIZ

Aging causes people to lose intelligence.

☐ TRUE

☐ FALSE

FALSE: According to WebMD getting older has its perks. For one, a person has what's called crystallized intelligence and it keeps getting better even when you're 65 or 70.*

(cited from https://www.webmd.com/healthy-aging/ss/slideshow-aging-surprises)

DAY 8
30-DAY CHALLENGE

PHONE AN OLD FRIEND

#WISEWOMANTIPS

STOP CALLING
YOURSELF
AN OLD
LADY.

! TRIVIA

WHO INVENTED THE SHELVES INSIDE REFRIGERATOR DOORS AND THE FOOT PEDAL TRASH CAN?

LILLIAN GILBRETH

53

The best advice I can give a woman as she grows older is to just keep living. Keep on living the best that you can. And yes, try to stay positive.

Gwen (100)

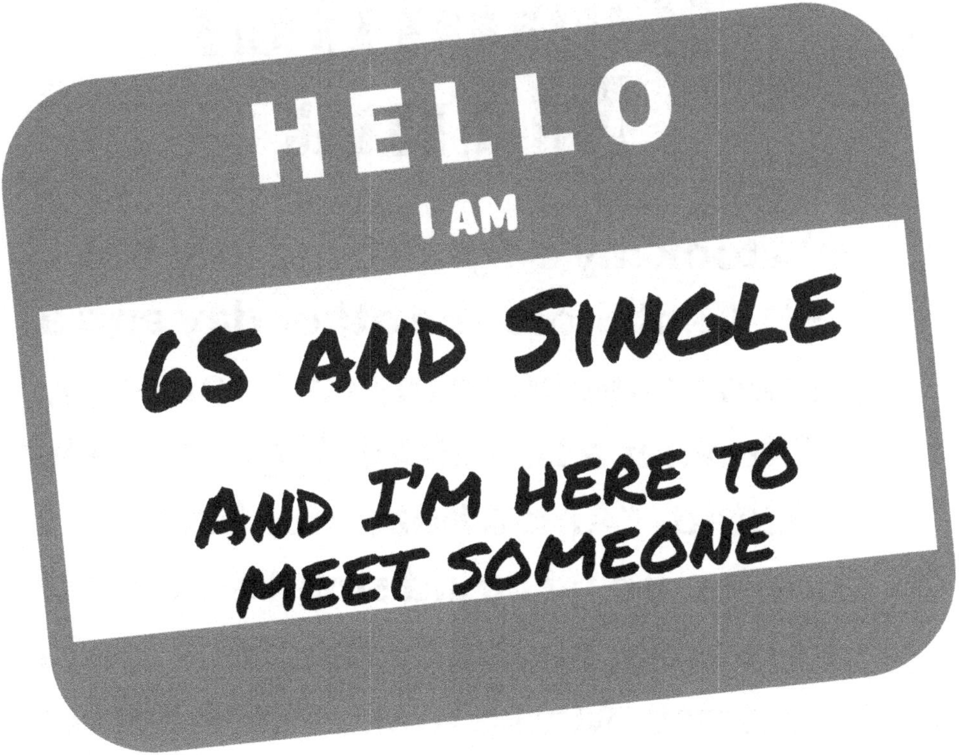
HELLO
I AM
65 AND SINGLE
AND I'M HERE TO
MEET SOMEONE

Beautiful Mama

I took my dog with me into the 99-Cent Store the other day and a man came up to my cart and said, "Oh what a beautiful dog." Then he added, "And a beautiful Mama." I don't care if I could smell alcohol on his breath, anybody that tells me I'm a pretty Mama makes me happy.

(Alice 75)

DAY 9
30-DAY CHALLENGE

THROW OUT ALL YOUR OLD MAKE-UP

Freida

Do you still get hot flashes?

Not too much anymore, why?

I was out to dinner last night and the waiter asked if I would like a towel.

58

I dream about...

... I believe strongly in getting a good haircut. I think sometimes women just let their hair go as they age and it looks terrible. Investing in someone who really does a good job cutting your hair is super important.

Sandi (69)

TAKE A CHANCE

Paint an accent wall in your home.

LOVE YOUR AGE

**Don't let time pass you by.
Keep it right by your side,
upfront and down the middle.**

I AM HAVING A SENIOR
MOMENT BUT I CANNOT
FOR THE LIFE OF ME
REMEMBER WHAT
IT IS

DAY 10
30-DAY CHALLENGE

DONATE YOUR USED BOOKS TO A LIBRARY

... I weigh myself every day. I have done this for the past 20 years. I am a bit OCD but I like to weigh around 130. So if I get on a scale and weigh 132 or 133 I don't eat much that day. I have been able to keep my weight steady as a result.

Marty (72)

TAKE A CHANCE

Buy a lottery ticket.

"

I think a smile goes a long way to improve my personal appearance.

Liz 67

**Can you share something
you wish you hadn't done
in your younger years?**

*Smoke and spend too much time in
the sun without a hat or sunscreen.*

Sandy (68)

DAY 11
30-DAY CHALLENGE

LIST
EVERYTHING
YOU
ARE
GRATEFUL
FOR

Freida

I'm not a big fan of health foods.

Really??? Why not???

At my age, I need all the preservatives I can get.

#WISEWOMANTIPS

IF YOU'RE SERIOUSLY DEPRESSED MAKE AN APPOINTMENT WITH YOUR DOCTOR.

POP QUIZ

Women tend to get angry and mean spirited as they age.

☐ TRUE

☐ FALSE

FALSE: *Actually women become happier and less inclined to get angry as they age. Scientists haven't figured out exactly why this happens, but they do have some theories. Older people might control their emotions better, and focus more on how to make the most of life.*

LOVE YOUR AGE

Start your day with a smile, a perfect stretch, and a set of stairs.

Every morning Sylvia wished she'd used Rogaine for the past 40 years like Frank. "Look at this guy with his full head of hair and thick beard... and me standing here with just the beard."

DAY 12
30-DAY CHALLENGE

CHANGE YOUR VACUUM AND WATER FILTERS

... I don't worry about the changes occurring as I age. Everyone earns their own wrinkles.

Rita (72)

!

TRIVIA

HOW MUCH TIME DO WOMEN SPEND OVER THEIR LIVES MENSTRUATING?

? ?

OVER 4 YEARS

I've had a lot of friends fall and break their leg or hip. When I walk I try to stay in the zone and make sure to note what's in front of me. Also, I am super conscious when stepping off a curb.

Joan Age 77

DAY 13
30-DAY CHALLENGE

GO A
DAY
WITHOUT
ALCOHOL
OR OTHER
SELF
MEDICATING
SUBSTANCE

Freida

I'm really good at multitasking.

Good skill to have.

Yes, I can laugh and pee at the same time.

"

Well, here I am in my seventies. I wish I had taken more time to absorb each day.

Betty 72

MY GLASS IS ALWAYS
FULL BECAUSE
I DON'T
FLOAT THE
OLIVES

DAY 14
30-DAY CHALLENGE

PARK YOUR CAR AWAY FROM AN ENTRANCE TO GET A LONGER WALK

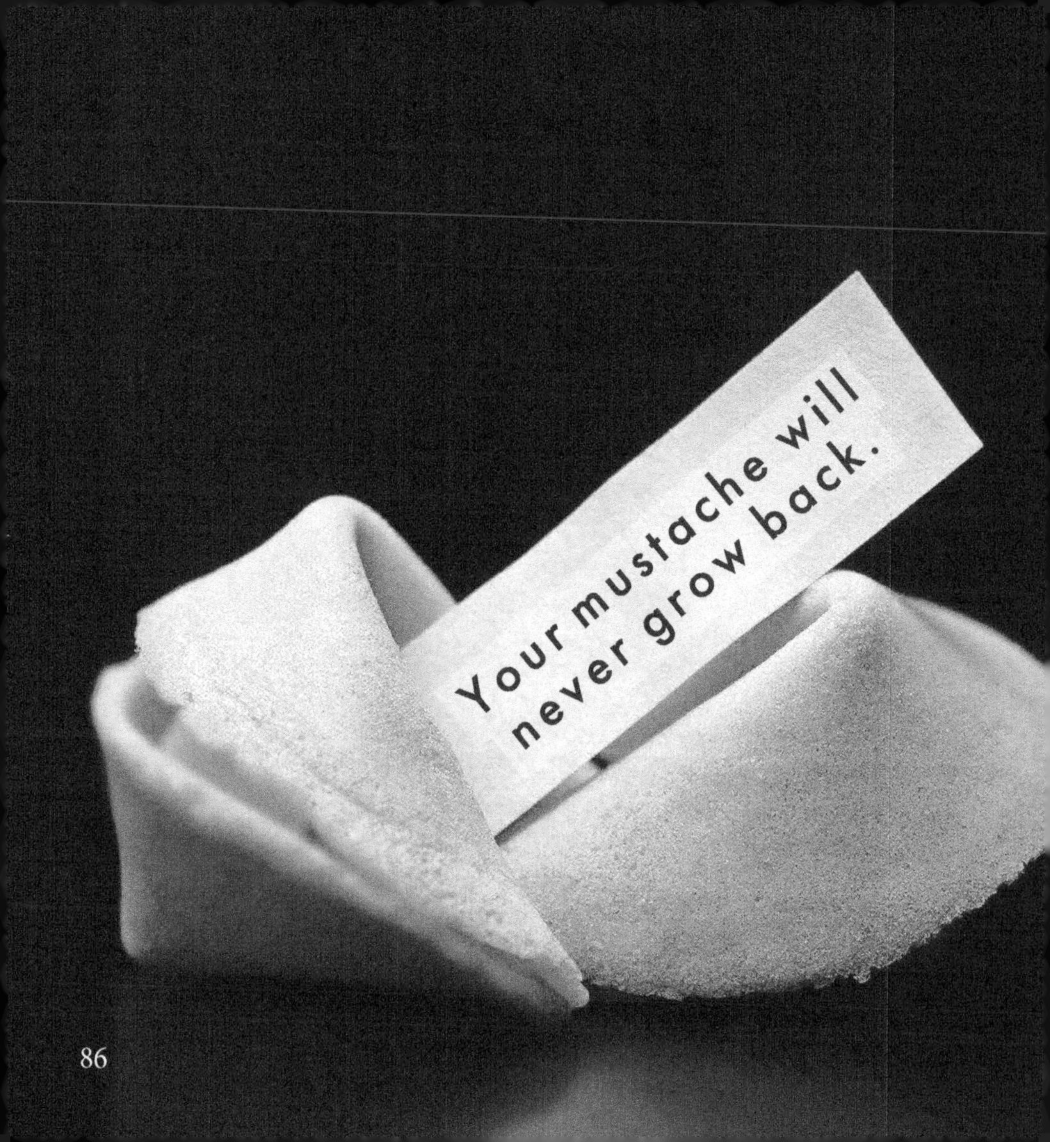
Your mustache will
never grow back.

#WISEWOMANTIPS

DON'T ADMIT TO BEING OLD. JUST KEEP GOING AND DOING.

LOVE YOUR AGE

Listening to the younger generation keeps your juices flowing. Create your own smoothie.

Can you share anything out of the ordinary that you do to keep your mind sharp?

I purchased a GED workbook and relearned things I used to know.

April (72)

Gladys thought getting a rescue dog would be exciting.
Little did she know that she'd be the one being rescued.

DAY 15
30-DAY CHALLENGE

DRINK SIX 8-OUNCE GLASSES OF WATER

When someone compliments you by saying, "You sure don't look your age," just say thank you and look in the mirror and mentally agree. Let your attitude reflect that you can be beautiful, sexy, vivacious, smart and talented at any age.

Sally (81)

!

WHO WAS THE FIRST WOMAN TO BE ELECTED TO CONGRESS?

TRIVIA

? ?

JEANNETTE RANKIN IN 1916

This or That?

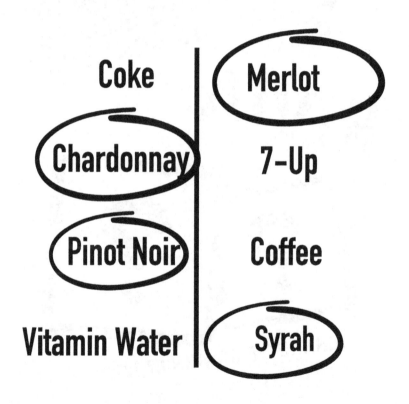

DAY 16
30-DAY CHALLENGE

MAKE
A LIST
OF 5
THINGS
YOU
WANT
TO CHANGE

Freida

I'm not sure why they call these the 'Golden Years'.

Why's that?

Cause my hair has turned to silver and I've got a lead butt.

TAKE A CHANCE

Register for an art class like pottery, painting, or drawing.

"

> *I just read that women who continue to have sex after 70 perform greater on cognitive tests than women who don't have sex very often. I am not surprised.*
> *(Roberta 70)*

... Everything doesn't have
to be perfect. I have a
new way of thinking and
it's called "pretty good".

Mary (65)

POP QUIZ

Women lose interest in sex as they grow old.

☐ TRUE

☐ FALSE

FALSE: While women have less sex as they age, their interest in sex remains high. Researchers also reveal that a woman's sexual satisfaction improves with age.

101

DAY 17
30-DAY CHALLENGE

DONATE CLOTHES YOU HAVEN'T WORN IN 2 YEARS

Clare and Janet decided it was time to have a chat with their friend, Delores. Her recycling habits were hurting the plan to recruit younger families into the neighborhood.

#WISEWOMANTIPS

IF POSSIBLE TRY
TO LEAVE THE
HOUSE AT LEAST
ONCE A DAY.

DON'T LET ANYONE EVER TRY TO GET YOUR

MONEY

... As a former educator I remember telling my students, if it doesn't get written down, it won't get done.

Chris (66)

LOVE YOUR AGE

Turn your pain into power and sweat your ass off now and then. It's liberating.

Do you have any advice for women regarding maintaining good health?

Spend time with people you appreciate and who are intellectually stimulating as well as kind, considerate, and sensitive.

Martha (75)

DAY 18
30-DAY CHALLENGE

GO A FULL DAY WITHOUT WATCHING TV

Your Beanie Baby collection is worth 1.2 million.

#WISEWOMANTIPS

ADVICE TO WOMEN [AND MEN]...
STASH SOME CASH SOMEWHERE IN
YOUR HOUSE JUST IN CASE OF AN
EARTHQUAKE, FIRE, FLOOD OR
WHATEVER. YOU WANT TO BE ABLE
TO HAVE SOME HARD-CORE CASH IN
CASE THE GRID GOES DOWN.

TAKE A CHANCE

Rearrange your furniture.

... It's always nice to have money and a lot of money is even nicer. But having a lot of LOVE in my life is more important.

Patty (67)

Since I've stopped working, I've learned to manage my time fairly well. I don't want anyone to take power over that. My time is more precious than anything.

JoAnn Age 66

FAQs

What do you know now in your 60s that you didn't know in your 20s and 30s?

I used to get bothered by things I thought at the time were huge and now they're just so insignificant. Life is a gift, and now I don't sweat the small stuff.

Marie (65)

DAY 19
30-DAY CHALLENGE

ELIMINATE
SOCIAL
MEDIA
FOR
A
DAY

Freida

Do you ever feel like you've had too much wine to drink?

No, never!

mee eider.

!

WHAT IS THE AVERAGE NUMBER OF WORDS SPOKEN PER DAY BY A WOMAN?

TRIVIA

20,000 (13,000 MORE THAN THE AVERAGE MAN)

"

If I were to offer any advice about getting older, I'd say get a dog if you can.

Joan 89

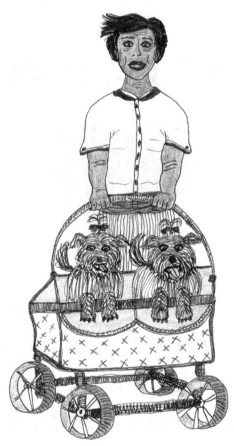

"Gramma in waiting" doing double duty.

LOVE YOUR AGE

**Learning from younger
women shows us just
how far we've come.
Celebrate their knowledge!**

Looking Good

I believe if something bothers you and you have the money or ability to fix it, then go for it. I get Botox which makes me feel more attractive and confident. I was pretty in my younger years and still think I look good which is important to me. It takes guts however to endure the pain as these Botox shots are nothing to sneeze at.
(Shelly 67)

DAY 20
30-DAY CHALLENGE

BUY
A
TOMATO
OR
PEPPER
PLANT

TAKE A CHANCE

Go to a restaurant by yourself.

#WISEWOMANTIPS

EVERY FIVE MINUTES AN OLDER WOMAN SLIPS AND FALLS IN HER HOME. THROW OUT YOUR THROW RUGS AND DON'T WALK AROUND THE HOUSE IN SLIPPERY SOCKS.

Tired of slipping on her high-gloss tiled floors, Betty harnessed her MacGyver instincts and designed some self-sticking padded slippers.

"

I don't want to feel young again.
It's taken me all this time to
realize that I like who I am.
(Barbara 64)

DON'T LET ANYONE EVER MAKE YOU FEEL

MARGINALIZED

POP QUIZ

Women who retire early live longer.

☐ **TRUE**

☐ **FALSE**

FALSE: Early retirement might not be the best thing for your health. A study called the Longevity Project found that people who work hard at a job they enjoy live the longest. That, along with good friends and a good marriage, could be the key to sticking around a while.

**Do you do anything special
to keep looking attractive?**

*I think a thin waist makes my clothes
look better so I exercise every day to
keep my waist small.*

Shelly (72)

I WISH THAT
EVERY DAY
WAS NATIONAL
HAPPY HOUR
DAY

DAY 21
30-DAY CHALLENGE

CALL YOUR LOCAL ELEMENTARY SCHOOL AND OFFER TO VOLUNTEER

HOW MUCH TIME OVER A WOMAN'S LIFE IS SPENT DECIDING WHAT TO WEAR?

TRIVIA

? ?

NEARLY ONE YEAR

I'm really glad I got a rescue dog.

He looks so much happier now than the first time I saw him.

He should be after all the $$$$ I've spent on him.

135

#WISEWOMANTIPS

DON'T BE SO QUICK TO SIGN UP FOR A HANDICAP PARKING PERMIT UNLESS YOU REALLY NEED IT. RESIST FOR AS LONG AS POSSIBLE.

"

I plan to work for as long as I can. Don't count me out just yet.

Carol 66

LOVE YOUR AGE

Wise women have so much to share. Enjoy a few seasoned secrets and then share your samples.

This or That?

High Heels | ⬭ Clogs

⬭ Sneakers | Thigh High Boots

⬭ Slippers | Wedgies

Stilettos | ⬭ Flip Flops

DAY 22
30-DAY CHALLENGE

TAKE
DIFFERENT
ROUTE
ON
YOUR
DAILY
WALK

... I have a secret stash of cash on hand. Why? Because it makes me feel independent from my husband.

Patricia (71)

Embrace those Beautiful Afternoons

Required to pass yet another eye exam to maintain her driving license at age 98, Lou decided to take matters into her own hands.

DAY 23
30-DAY CHALLENGE

BUY A
2-POUND
BARBEL
AND START
WORKING
OUT

Women should be thinking about how prepared they are to be alone. Try to visualize what you might need as you get along in age. For example, right now I'm looking at different nursing homes so if anything goes wrong, I'll be in a good place. You have to think ahead and not let things surprise you.

Joan (89)

TAKE A
CHANCE

Get a tiny
tattoo.

POP QUIZ

Aging causes a person to get shorter.

☐ TRUE

☐ FALSE

TRUE: As you grow older, gravity has its effects on the body. The spaces between the bones in your spine -- called vertebrae -- get closer together. That can make you about an inch shorter as you get older. Yoga and stretching exercises can help to reduce any associated pain.

**What are you currently doing
to influence your health?**

*Well, I still run. But not as far as I
used to. I can run four miles a day.
I think that helps.*

Anna (73)

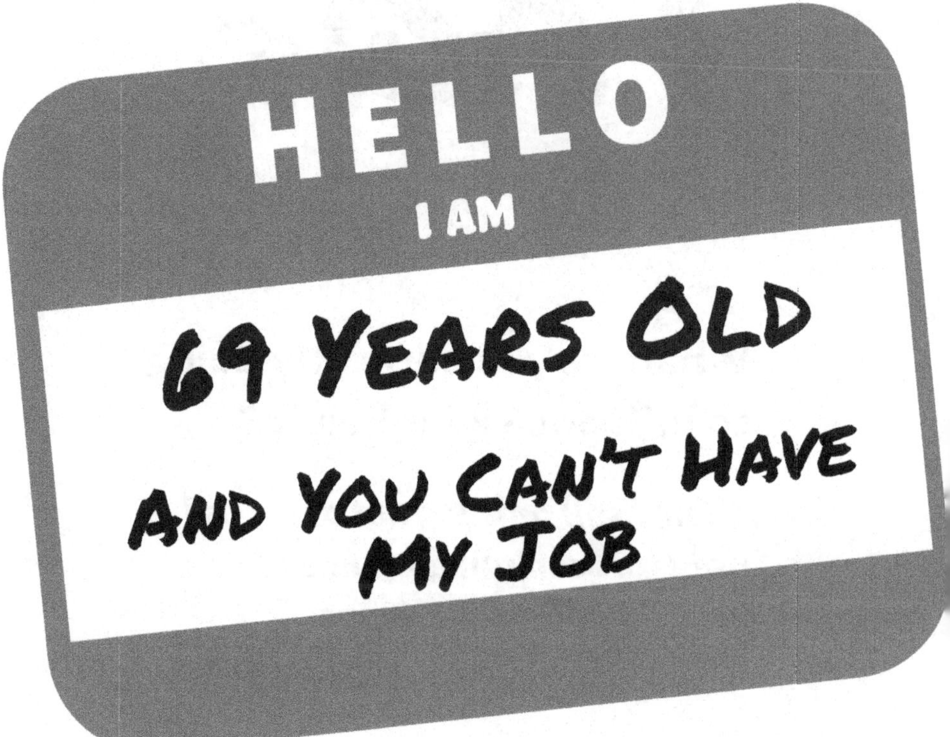
HELLO
I AM
69 YEARS OLD
AND YOU CAN'T HAVE MY JOB

DAY 24
30-DAY CHALLENGE

JOIN

AN

OFFICIAL

GROUP

Freida

> Whenever I ask my kids for help with my iPhone they laugh and say I should just learn the functions.

Same thing here.

> Just wait till they ask me how to cook their 24 lb turkey in the microwave this Thanksgiving.

152

#WISEWOMANTIPS

IF YOU HAVE TROUBLE REMEMBERING THINGS NOW AND THEN, REPEAT WHAT YOU WANT TO REMEMBER A FEW TIMES RIGHT AFTER HEARING IT. FOR EXAMPLE, WHEN INTRODUCED TO SOMEONE, SAY THEIR NAME TWO OR THREE TIMES IN THE CONVERSATION.

MY DREAM
IS TO MAKE
JULIA CHILD'S

B E E F

BOURGUIGNON

LOVE YOUR AGE

Turn this day into something spectacular. Make it one you will remember tomorrow.

These tech companies are finally getting smart, Rita thought. Including a tech guy in the box with my new computer was pure genius. Now all I have to do is prepare the guest room and plan a dinner for two.

ON AVERAGE, HOW MANY TIMES A YEAR DOES A WOMAN CRY?

TRIVIA

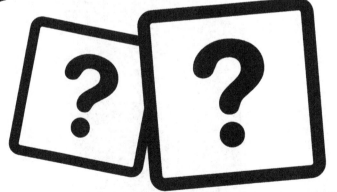

BETWEEN 30–64 TIMES

DAY 25
30-DAY CHALLENGE

MAKE
THAT
DOCTOR
OR
DENTIST
APPOINTMENT

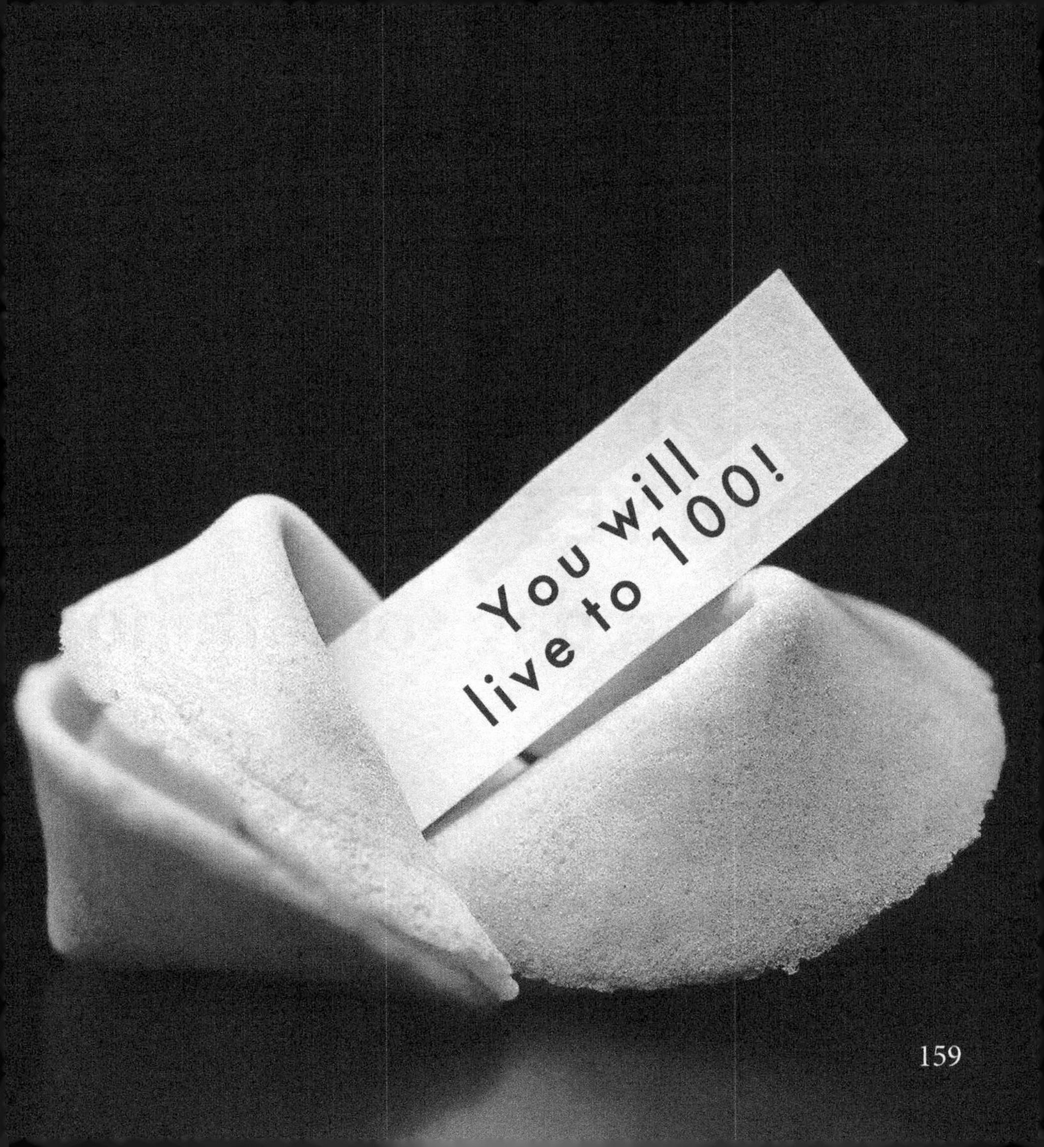
You will
live to 100!

... I'm in my mid-70s and YES on any given day something hurts.

Fay (75)

"

I didn't know life would go by so quickly. I still feel like I'm in my 30s.

Stephanie 60

As a beautician what products do you think help a woman as she ages?

The girl working the make-up counter is only there to sell you products not to help you. Moisturizer is all we need, any kind, and the cheaper the better.

Anna (73)

DAY 26
30-DAY CHALLENGE

GROW
A HERB
GARDEN

HOW MANY
GUMMY
VITAMINS DID
YOU TAKE
TODAY?

Freida

It's funny how things change when you get older.

Like what?

Well, I used to take drugs to stay awake but now I take them to fall asleep!

#WISEWOMANTIPS

MAINTAINING A GOOD LEVEL OF VITAMIN D IS ONE OF THE CHEAPEST WAYS TO IMPROVE YOUR HEALTH AND LIFE EXPECTANCY. GO OUTSIDE FOR AT LEAST 15-30 MINUTES A DAY. VITAMIN D CAN ALSO IMPACT LEVELS OF DEPRESSION AND MAKE YOU FEEL HAPPIER.

The average woman carries approximately 38 items in her purse. Can you find the item that does not belong in a purse?

This or That?

Poached Egg | (Pancakes)

(Blintzes) | Oatmeal

(French Toast) | Fruit Cup

Dry Toast | (Scones)

DAY 27

30-DAY CHALLENGE

GET A

BETA

FISH

I would advise women to think about a plan to walk into before actually retiring. Don't think that travel and remodeling a kitchen will satisfy all your needs especially if you've been in a high-impact career. I felt like I was getting off a treadmill and spinning out of control. Those were some tough years for me. Get a plan.

Shelly (72)

TAKE A CHANCE

Change the color
of your hair.

How do you keep up with the changing world?

You can't just do what you did 30 years ago and then grow in this world. Things move pretty fast now. You need to keep up with what's going on through reading, watching the news or attending webinars.

Betty (70)

BRING ON
ANOTHER
BIRTHDAY. I CAN
HANDLE
IT!

DAY 28
30-DAY CHALLENGE

LEARN
A NEW
TECH
SKILL

TAKE A CHANCE

Paint your front door your favorite color.

The bouffant will come back in style.

Freida

I am diving into a deep depression.

Oh no! Why?

Outlander, Ray Donovan, and the Ozarks are over for the seaon!

#WISEWOMANTIPS

LAUGHING LOWERS BLOOD PRESSURE AND CAN TRIGGER THE RELEASE OF ENDORPHIN. LAUGHING AT OUR OWN MISTAKES IS THE BEST. MAKE FUN OF YOURSELF BECAUSE PEOPLE WITH A SENSE OF HUMOR TEND TO LIVE LONGER.

... If I have one fear as I age, it's that I won't be able to fit in all I want to see and do before my time is up, so I always plan activities while I can still do them.

Mary Anne (68)

Sometimes it's a shock to look in the mirror and say, "Hi Mom." You still think you're 35 and you think, Oh my God. How did 81 happen?"

Suzie Age 81

POP QUIZ

A person's grip becomes weaker as they age.

☐ TRUE

☐ FALSE

TRUE: A person's grip gets weaker over time which is probably caused by brittle bones, arthritis, or muscle loss. You can do many exercises to help such as squeezing a tennis ball as hard as you can for 3 to 5 seconds, then resting briefly. Start with once a day or once every other day, depending on how your hands feel.

Slightly panicked about her new job at city hall, Amy reached out to her grandson to learn how to make an Excel speadsheet.

DAY 29
30-DAY CHALLENGE

VISIT
YOUR
LOCAL
SENIOR
CENTER

... I have what I call the 'three-day rule' when something hurts. If something doesn't stop hurting in three days then I call my doctor. An exception of course is excruciating pain.

Susan (67)

TAKE A CHANCE

Test drive a sports car just for fun.

FAQs

How do you manage to stay so happy?

For me, "A day without smiling is a day without sunshine." I believe it's true. Smiling makes me feel happy and even happier if the smile is returned.

Monica (81)

DAY 30
30-DAY CHALLENGE

MAKE SOMETHING CREATIVE WITH YOUR HANDS

... I don't fear
anything right now.
I feel the same as
I did 20 years ago.

Frannie (100)

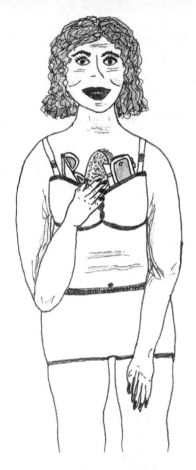

Linda got really tired of leaving her purse behind at the grocery store.

Enjoy additional books from our Sister to Sister Series

www.sistertosistersecrets.com

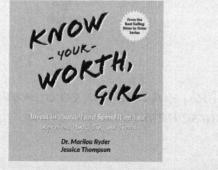

Made in the USA
Coppell, TX
06 April 2022